ADOPTION
—AND—
DISCLOSURE

A REVIEW OF THE LAW

By Madelyn DeWoody

CHILD WELFARE LEAGUE OF AMERICA

CHILD WELFARE LEAGUE OF AMERICA, INC.
440 First Street, NW, Suite 310, Washington, DC 20001-2085

CURRENT PRINTING (last digit)
10 9 8 7 6 5 4 3 2 1

Cover and text design by Jennifer Riggs

Printed in the United States of America
ISBN # 0–878678–577–4

CONTENTS

Acknowledgments

The author wishes to thank the following individuals who contributed significantly to this project: Mark Lesko, whose extensive legal research formed the basis of this report; Debra Diener and Adrienne Hyat for their editorial assistance; Nickola Dixon for her essential word processing expertise; and Mary Liepold for her editing.

INTRODUCTION

Over the last decade, adoption agencies have increasingly faced issues related to obtaining and disclosing information about the medical and social history of an adopted child and the child's birth family. Quality practice supports sharing of information so that children with medical, psychological, and developmental problems are placed with families prepared to meet their needs; children receive prompt and appropriate diagnostic and treatment services for physical, emotional, and genetic disorders; adoptive families are financially and emotionally prepared to care for the children placed with them; and all members of the adoption triad—child, birth family, and adoptive family—have access to health and other background information that may have importance for them throughout their lives.

Issues surrounding the disclosure of nonidentifying health and background information have surfaced both in the courts and in the statutory reform efforts of a number of states. Courts have begun to consider the scope of the duty of adoption agencies to obtain and disclose nonidentifying information and have found agencies liable for money damages when that duty is breached. Similarly, state legislatures have begun to define, through state law, the disclosure obligations of adoption agencies as well as the sanctions that flow from failure to comply with those requirements. Adoption agencies must understand the judicial decisions and statutory requirements in this area. Full and open disclosure prior to or at the time of adoptive placement is not only a matter of best practice, but also a matter of avoiding potential liability.

In this overview of the legal developments around disclosure of health and background information in adoption, part one reviews the major court decisions in this area and summarizes the judicial trends. Part two reviews statutory law regarding such disclosure and charts the various ways in which states have defined the nature and scope of the duty to disclose nonidentifying information.

THE COURTS: THE TORT OF "WRONGFUL ADOPTION"

Wrongful adoption, as a new basis for lawsuits against adoption agencies, is a legal development with significant implications for public and voluntary child welfare agencies. Through lawsuits alleging "wrongful adoption," a number of adoptive parents have succeeded in obtaining monetary awards from adoption agencies based on court findings that the agency failed to disclose or misrepresented the health status or background of an adopted child at the time the child was placed. Before 1986, the only remedy adoptive parents could pursue against adoption agencies for misrepresentation regarding a child's health or background was to annul the adoption,[1] an alternative that many adoptive parents did not wish to seek and which, consequently, was rarely used. In 1986, however, the Ohio Supreme Court, in *Burr v. Board of County Commissioners*,[2] ruled for the first time that "wrongful adoption" was a valid cause of action for adoptive parents against adoption agencies under which parents could recover monetary damages. Since the court's decision in *Burr*, two other states— California and Minnesota—have allowed similar lawsuits that permit adoptive parents to recover damages. This trend is likely to continue, with additional states finding agencies potentially liable under theories of "wrongful adoption."

As the following discussion of the major "wrongful adoption" cases illustrates, three major liability theories are emerging from court decisions. Agencies will be liable if, prior to or at the time of the adoptive placement, they engage in: (1) intentional misrepresentation, that is, a deliberate misrepresentation regarding a child's health or background; (2) deliberate concealment, that is, intentional failure to communicate a known material fact about the child's health or background; or (3) negligent disclosure of information, that is, a voluntary offer of inaccurate information about a child's health or background. It is also likely that agencies can be held liable if they negligently fail to communicate genetic or medical background information when undertaking to disclose some, but not all of such information. The emergence and ongoing development of the tort of wrongful adoption clearly provides adoptive parents with the right to recover monetary damages against agencies on the basis of certain conduct involving disclosure or nondisclosure of information related to the child's health or background. The trend, however, has also led to the development of specific limits on the kinds of conduct for which an agency may be found liable. Agencies should be aware of the practices that may expose them to liability so that policy and practice in the area of disclosure meet the standard of conduct expected by courts.

When Is an Adoption Agency Liable?

The three major wrongful adoption cases decided by courts thus far provide a basis for understanding the type of conduct that may lead to agency liability in relation to disclosure of an adoptive child's health and background information. In each of these cases, adoptive parents sought money damages and did not seek to annul the adoption. The three cases—*Burr v. Board of County Commissioners, Michael J. v. Los Angeles County Department of Adoptions,* and *M.H. and J.L.H. v. Caritas Family Services*—will be discussed in detail.

1. *Burr v. Board of County Commissioners*

In *Burr,* the first case recognizing wrongful adoption as a cause of action, Russell and Betty Burr adopted a 17-month-old boy through the county child welfare department. Department case-workers informed the Burrs in 1964 that the child was a "nice big, healthy baby boy" born in the local city hospital.[3] The Burrs were also told that the child's mother was an unmarried 18-year-old who had been living with her parents; the grandparents were "mean" to the child; and the mother had decided to move away to seek better employment and to surrender the child for adoption.[4] After the Burrs adopted the child, Patrick, he began to show signs of significant physical and mental problems: a speech impediment, poor motor skills, and learning disabilities, which, as he entered primary school, led to a classification of EMR (educable mentally retarded). By high school, Patrick's condition had deteriorated. Ultimately, he was diagnosed as suffering from Huntington's Chorea, a genetically inherited disease that destroys the central nervous system.

During Patrick's treatment for his condition, the Burrs succeeded in obtaining a court order opening the sealed adoption records that described the child's background before adoption. The records revealed that the representations made by the caseworkers in 1964 had been false. Patrick's mother was actually a 31-year-old patient at the state psychiatric hospital; Patrick had not been born at the city hospital but had been delivered at the state institution for persons with mental illness; and although the identity of Patrick's father was unknown, it was presumed that he too had a mental illness. The records also revealed that Patrick's biological mother functioned at a low intellectual level, suffered from a speech impediment, and had been diagnosed as "mild mental deficiency, idiopathic, with psychotic reactions."[5] The Burrs learned that much of the information they had been given was completely fictitious: that the grandparents were "mean," that the mother was moving to another location, and all the information about Patrick except his sex and age. At the same time, they learned much about Patrick's background that had not been shared with them at the time of the adoption: he had suffered a fever at birth; psychological assessments indicated he was functioning at a lower intellectual level than his chronological age; and it had been recommended that Patrick be assessed in the future for evidence of social and emotional developmental problems.

After the Burrs discovered that Patrick's family and personal background had been misrepresented to them, they sued the adoption agency, seeking monetary damages for Patrick's medical and other expenses as well as damages for their own emotional pain and suffering. The trial court made an award of $125,000 to the Burrs. The Supreme Court of Ohio upheld the award, finding that the couple had a cause of action for wrongful adoption based on the agency's "deliberate act of misinforming the Burrs, which, in effect, made them the victims of fraud."[6] The court's decision found that the agency's conduct met the legal elements of fraud:

1. a representation,

2. which is material to the transaction,

3. made falsely, with knowledge of its falsity or with such utter disregard and recklessness as to whether it is true or false that knowledge may be inferred,

4. with the intent of misleading another into relying upon it;

5. justifiable reliance upon the representation or concealment; and

6. a resulting injury proximately caused by the reliance.

The court found ample evidence of each legal element. The court noted that the agency had knowingly made false statements about Patrick's background, including the statement that the baby was nice and healthy when, in fact, the agency had test records showing, among other things, that the child had low intelligence and was at risk of emotional problems; the representations that he was born at the city hospital and that his mother was an unwed 18-year-old living with her parents; and fictitious statements that the grandparents were "mean" to the boy and that the mother was moving away. These misrepresentations were found to be material to the adoption and, according to the court, were "obviously made with the intention of misleading the Burrs into relying upon them as fact while making their decision whether to adopt."[7] The court also noted that the Burrs had testified that they would not have adopted Patrick had they known the truth about his history. Considering all the evidence, the court concluded that the agency knew the actual history of the child, intended that the Burrs rely on their representations, and "in fact misled the Burrs to their detriment," a justifiable reliance that led to the expenses they sought to have compensated.[8]

The court, however, drew a careful line between the agency's deliberate act of misinforming the Burrs and its failure to disclose known information about Patrick's background:

> *It is not mere failure to disclose the risks inherent in this child's background which we hold to be actionable. Rather, it is the deliberate act of misinforming this couple which deprived them of their right to make a sound parenting decision and which led to the compensable injuries.*[9]

The *Burr* court was clear that deliberate misrepresentations will result in agency liability. It, however, left open the question whether nondisclosure of information alone could result in a determination of agency liability.

2. *Michael J. v. Los Angeles County Department of Adoptions*

In *Michael J. v. Los Angeles County Department of Adoptions*,[10] the California Court of Appeals followed the lead of the Ohio Supreme Court, and, for the first time under California law, allowed recovery for an adoptive parent under a theory of wrongful adoption. Michael, the adopted child, had been born with a port wine stain, a large reddish birthmark, on his upper body and face. Michael was considered a "hard to place" child and was featured on a television program in the hope of locating a prospective adoptive parent for him. Mary Trout contacted the county adoption agency in response to the program. She asked about the port wine stain but was told that it was "merely a birthmark."[11] In reality, it was symptomatic of Sturge-Weber Syndrome, a congenital condition often associated with mental retardation and epilepsy. The records of the county, in fact, stated: "Medically this has been described as a 'port wine stain' which will probably not fade as the baby grows older. However, doctor will not make a definite statement as to the prognosis for this child."[12] The information related to Michael's prognosis was not conveyed to Ms. Trout.

Eleven years after Ms. Trout adopted Michael, he had an epileptic seizure and was diagnosed as having Sturge-Weber Syndrome. She brought suit against the adoption agency, claiming that on the basis of medical knowledge and information available at the time of Michael's adoption, the county knew or should have known in the exercise of reasonable care that the port wine stain was a manifestation of Sturge-Weber Syndrome.[13] She sued on two legal bases, fraud and negligence.

The California court considered each legal basis separately in deciding the type of conduct that would result in a determination of agency liability with regard to disclosure of information about a child's background. First, the court followed the Ohio court's decision in *Burr* and ruled that an agency can be held liable for fraud. In *Michael J.*, however, the court went beyond finding liability for an affirmative misrepresentation, as the court did in *Burr,* and held that "the failure to disclose a material fact within the agency's possession—that the examining physician would not render a prognosis for Michael...at the very least suggests that the nondisclosure was fraudulent."[14] The rule, according to the *Michael J.* court, is that "there must be a good faith full disclosure of material facts concerning existing or past conditions of a child's health."[15] The California court held that nondisclosure of a known material fact was conduct that could result in liability under a theory of fraud.

Second, the court considered, and rejected, the argument that an agency could be liable for negligence in the process of disclosing information about a child's health or background. The court held firm to the rule that:

...an adoption agency cannot be made the guarantor of an infant's future good health and should not be liable for mere negligence in providing information regarding the health of prospective adoptee... By recognizing an action for intentional misrepresentation or fraudulent concealment, we are not imposing on the agency a duty to predict the future health of a prospective adoptee.[16]

Like the court in *Burr*, the California court refused to impose liability for simple negligence, that is, mere inadvertence or carelessness, but required instead that the agency *intend* to misrepresent or conceal material information.

3. *M.H. and J.L.H. v. Caritas Family Services*

The third major case, *M.H. and J.L.H. v. Caritas Family Services*,[17] was decided by the Minnesota Supreme Court. In *M.H.*, the plaintiffs contacted an adoption agency and, in a conversation with a social worker regarding a particular child, were informed there was a possibility of incest in the child's family. When the couple met the child, the social worker asked if it mattered to them whether there was incest in the family background, and they responded that it did not. The couple did not inquire specifically when the incest had occurred, and apparently did not consider the possibility that incest accounted for the child's conception. The social worker offered no further information, nor did the written information given to the adoptive couple mention incest. The information, instead, described the child's biological father as in "good health" and of "normal intelligence."

Soon after the adoption, it became apparent that the child had difficulties. He was jumpy and easily agitated. Problems continued to develop, including such behavior as setting fire to the furniture in the home. The boy was diagnosed as suffering from attention deficit hyperactivity disorder, and medication and counseling were begun. It was only upon seeking to adopt a second child that the couple learned that the natural parents of their first adopted child were siblings and that the birth father was, in reality, considered borderline hyperactive and of low average intelligence and had required mental health counseling as a child.

In their suit, the adoptive couple sought to recover damages based on a claim for negligent misrepresentation, a basis previously rejected in *Burr* and *Michael J.* The Minnesota Supreme Court held that adoptive parents may bring a lawsuit based on negligent misrepresentation against an adoption agency.[18] The court held that a negligent misrepresentation action may be brought when an agency, having undertaken to disclose information about a child's genetic parents and medical background, negligently withholds information in such a way that adoptive parents are misled. However, the court emphasized the agency's voluntary assumption of a duty to disclose. As the court of appeals held in *M.H.*:

> *The cause of action [for negligent misrepresentation] is...limited to those situations where the agency assumes a duty to inform prospective parents about the child's health or the health of the natural parents. The adoptive parents may recover only those extraordinary expenses incurred as a result of the misrepresentations, not all the ordinary expenses of raising a child.*[19]

The court also considered the adoptive parents' claim that the agency had engaged in intentional misrepresentation when it failed to disclose the nature of the incest involved. The court rejected that theory, finding that there were no facts or evidence to suggest that the adoption agency intended to mislead the adoptive parents by withholding the full facts regarding incest in the child's background. The court noted that "the evidence suggests the opposite: if Caritas intended to mislead plaintiffs, it is unlikely it would have raised the question of incest with them at all."[20]

Potential Agency Liability: Three Categories

In summary, courts have found adoption agencies legally liable under a theory of "wrongful adoption" for several types of conduct:

1. Intentional Misrepresentation: Deliberate Misrepresentation about a Child's Health or Background

In cases based on this theory, the important facts that lead to liability are: a definite statement is made about a matter of importance to the adoption, specifically, the child's health and background; the agency knows the statement is false or strongly suspects, on the basis of other information, that the information is false; the agency knows that the adoptive parent will rely on the statement in deciding whether to adopt the child; the adoptive parent actually does rely on the statement in making the decision to adopt; and the adoptive parent is harmed in some way—often by incurring large and unexpected medical expenses in caring for the child—as a result of relying on the agency's statements about the child's health or background. As illustrated by *Burr*, an intentional misrepresentation may include descriptions of a child as "nice and healthy" when information to the contrary is known or descriptions of a birth mother as a healthy 18-year-old when the agency knows that she is, in reality, beyond her teens and a patient at a psychiatric facility.

2. Deliberate Concealment: Intentional Failure to Disclose a Known Material Fact about the Child's Health or Background

In cases based on this theory, the important facts that lead to liability are: the agency knows information about the child's health or background; the information is "material," that is, it is important to a potential adoptive parent's decision to adopt the child; the agency does not provide the potential adoptive parent with the information; the agency knows that the potential adoptive parent relies on it for such information; the potential adoptive parent goes forward with the adoption based on the information that is shared; and the adoptive parent is harmed, usually through incurring unexpected expenses related to the care of the child, as a result.

Examples of deliberate concealment may include situations in which an agency knows that the child has tested positive for the human immunodeficiency virus (HIV) or knows that a child suffered oxygen deprivation at birth, but fails to share this information with potential adoptive parents.

3. Negligent Disclosure of Information Regarding the Child's History or Prognosis: Voluntary Provision of Inaccurate Information about a Child's Health or Background

In cases based on this theory, the important facts that lead to liability are: the agency voluntarily shares information about a child's history or prognosis; the information is not accurate and the agency would be expected to provide accurate information under the circumstances; the information causes the adoptive parent to go forward with the adoption; and the adoptive parent is harmed, usually through incurring unexpected expenses related to the care of the child, as a result.

Examples of negligent disclosure may include situations in which an adoption agency voluntarily informs potential adoptive parents about the medical or developmental implications of a child's condition or the risks associated with a family history of a disease and that information is inaccurate.

Another Potential Category of Liability

In addition to potential liability for negligent disclosure of information, an agency may face liability for negligently withholding material information regarding a child's history or prognosis after it voluntarily undertakes to share such information, so that adoptive parents are misled. A few courts have considered this issue and have found that agencies can be held liable under such circumstances.

The important facts that lead to liability in these situations are: the agency voluntarily shares information about a child's history; the agency has information that is "material," that is, important to the decision to adopt; the agency does not share certain information with the adoptive parent; the withholding of the information misleads the adoptive parent; and the adoptive parent is harmed, usually through incurring unexpected expenses related to the care of the child.

An example of negligent withholding is a situation in which an adoption agency shares information about a child's family history of a disease, such as Huntington's Disease, and in the course of the discussion, provides incorrect information about the child's risk of contracting the disease. Failure to explain that there is no definitive test for a predisposition to contract the disease could constitute a negligent withholding of material information.

It should be noted that as case law has developed to this point, adoption agencies will not be liable for simply failing to disclose health information. Courts consistently have refused to impose liability based on a general duty on the part of adoption agencies to discover and disclose information about a child's health or background. However, if an agency chooses to share information and does so, the agency must use due care in providing full and accurate information or face potential liability.

When an Agency Is Liable, What Are the Damages?

When courts have found that an agency is liable, they generally have allowed adoptive parents to recover medical expenses they incur as a result of the child's condition. In *Burr,* for example, the adoptive parents recovered a total of $125,000 in damages, of which $80,000 was for medical treatment for Patrick. When liability is established, extraordinary medical expenses can generally be recovered.

Recovery for other types of damages has not been as consistent. In many cases, courts have refused to allow the adoptive parents to recover the expenses ordinarily incurred in the adoption of a child, holding, as did one court, that "it is only the extraordinary expenses, the unexpected expenses" resulting from a child's special needs that can be recovered.[21] Although the court in *Burr* allowed recovery for "other expenses and [the Burrs'] emotional damage,"[22] other courts have rejected adoptive parents' claim to damages for their emotional distress. In some states, an individual may recover for emotional distress that is negligently, in contrast to deliberately, inflicted only if the emotional distress is accompanied by physical injury.[23] When adoptive parents do not suffer any physical harm as a result of the agency's alleged negligence, courts may dismiss claims for emotional distress, noting, as one court did:

> *The distress that is usually experienced by close relatives when illness strikes a family member is normal and is not compensable.*[24]

This approach, however, is not consistently followed. In *M.H.,* for example, the court of appeals held that the trial court should have permitted the adoptive parent to add a claim for negligent infliction of emotional distress. Under Minnesota law, proof of resulting physical injuries is not required for a claim of emotional distress if there is a "direct invasion of rights."[25] The court held that negligent misrepresentation was a direct invasion of rights, and, therefore, the adoptive parents could pursue their emotional distress claim.[26]

References

[1] Comment, "The Emergence of Wrongful Adoption as a Cause of Action," *Journal of Family Law* 27 (1988-89), 475, 476, 480-81.

[2] 23 Ohio St. 3d 69, 491 N.E. 2d 1101 (1986).

[3] 491 N.E. 2d at 1103.

[4] 491 N.E. 2d at 1103.

[5] 491 N.E. 2d at 1104.

[6] 491 N.W. 2d at 1106.

[7] 491 N.W. 2d at 1106.

[8] 491 N.W. 2d at 1109.

[9]   491 N.W. 2d at 1109.

[10] 201 California App. 3d 859, 247 Cal. Rptr. 504 (1988).

[11] 201 California App. 3d at 875.

[12] 201 California App. 3d at 864.

[13] 201 California App. 3d at 863.

[14] 201 California App. 3d at 875.

[15] 201 California App. 3d at 875.

[16] 201 California App. 3d at 874-875.

[17] 488 N.W. 2d 282 (Minn. 1992).

[18] 488 N.W. 2d at 284.

[19] 475 N.W. 2d 94 98 (Minn. Ct. App. 1991).

[20] 488 N.W. 2d at 286.

[21] *Merakle v. Children's Service Society of Wisconsin,* 149 Wis. 2d, 19, 437 N.W. 2d 532, 534-35 (1989).

[22] 491 N.E. 2d at 1108.

[23] 437 N.W. 2d at 532.

[24] 437 N.W. 2d at 536.

[25] 475 N.W. 2d at 100.

[26] 475 N.W. 2d at 100.

STATE STATUTES: REQUIREMENTS FOR DISCLOSURE OF NONIDENTIFYING INFORMATION

In addition to court decisions that define the standards of conduct to which agencies must adhere, states also have defined in statute certain requirements related to disclosure of information about an adoptive child's health or background. These requirements may be more extensive and more stringent than those developed by the courts. State statutes generally impose duties that extend beyond disclosure to prospective adoptive parents, the focus of most court decisions, and require adoption agencies to collect and disclose specific types of information to a range of individuals.

Adoption agencies should be aware of all statutory requirements imposed by the states in which they provide services. In determining the requirements for disclosure under any particular state's law, it is essential to consult with an attorney licensed to practice in the state. The following information is provided as a guide only and is not intended to be either a complete statement or an interpretation of any state's law. The information and tables are offered to illustrate the types of requirements that are included in state law and to guide adoption agencies in their exploration of the statutory requirements that exist in their respective states.

Mandatory versus Discretionary Disclosure

Under most states' laws, certain health and background information regarding a child must be provided to certain individuals who are identified in the statute. Table 1 lists the states that require disclosure of certain types of nonidentifying information and identifies the state statute that addresses the mandatory disclosure requirement. Some states, rather than mandating disclosure, leave such decisions to the discretion of the public or the private adoption agency. These states are listed in Table 2. Finally, a few states, listed in Table 3, give courts the discretion to decide whether information will be disclosed.

Applicability of Disclosure Requirements to Different Types of Adoption

Most states that mandate disclosure of certain information require that disclosure take place for all adoptions: public and private agency adoptions and independent adoptions. Some states, however, as listed in Table 4, require disclosure of information only for adoptions by state and private agencies. Other states, as listed in Table 5, exclude all stepparent or relative adoptions from coverage of the mandatory disclosure laws.

Persons Entitled to Disclosure

State statutes show considerable variation in the categories of individuals who are entitled to disclosure of nonidentifying information.

Adoptive Parents and Legal Guardians

Most states, as listed in Table 1, require disclosure of health and background information to adoptive and prospective adoptive parents. Other states, in addition to those listed in Table 1, permit disclosure to adoptive and prospective adoptive parents and to legal guardians when such individuals seek health and background information. These states are listed in Tables 6 and 7.

Adopted Persons

States statutes vary in the requirements regarding disclosure of nonidentifying health and background information to adopted persons. Most states require that information related to the adopted person's health and background be disclosed to the adopted individual, but other states allow release of information only upon a court order or at the discretion of the adoption agency. Some states have not yet put this requirement into statute. Tables 8 and 9 provide information on each of the states' requirements regarding disclosure to adopted persons. Table 10 lists the 11 states with no such provisions.

Other Individuals

Some states extend access to relevant health and background information to certain other individuals under certain circumstances. Table 11 identifies states that have permitted disclosure of nonidentifying information to individuals other than adoptive parents, legal guardians, and adoptees.

Collection of Nonidentifying Information

States vary as to the entity that is assigned the responsibility for the collection of the adopted child's health and background information. In most cases, but not all, the responsibility rests with the child-placing agency. Table 12 provides each state's requirement.

Information That Must Be Collected and Disclosed

States show considerable variability in the type of information that must be collected and disclosed. Information categories include the child's medical history, other background information on the child, the biological family's medical history, the child's social and/or educational history, and the biological family's social and educational background.

The Child's Medical History

Most states require that the child's medical history be obtained and transmitted to persons entitled to disclosure. Table 13 identifies states whose statutes make reference to disclosure of the medical history of the child and Table 14 identifies states that make no such reference. Table 15 identifies states whose statutes specify certain types of information that must be gathered and disclosed.

The Medical and Genetic History of the Parents and the Biological Family

Most states require that the medical history of the birth parents be collected and disclosed. Fewer states require collection and disclosure of other biological relatives' medical history and even fewer specify that a genetic history be collected and disclosed. Table 16 identifies the statutory requirements for each state.

Social and Educational History

Some states require that a child's social history be obtained and disclosed. Only three states currently require that an educational history be obtained and disclosed. These states are listed in Table 17. Only a few states require that the social history of biological parents and ancestors be disclosed. Table 18 summarizes this information.

The Duty to Investigate

State statutes generally provide minimal guidance regarding the extent to which adoption agencies must investigate the medical history and background of children or their birth families. Table 19 sets forth the requirements of those states that have placed the duty to obtain such information on adoption agencies, which are then expected to work with parents or other guardians to obtain the necessary information. Table 20 identifies states whose statutes place the duty to supply information on persons or entities other than adoption agencies.

Collection and Retention of Information and Disclosure of Nonidentifying Information

Some states impose specific requirements on the collection and disclosure of nonidentifying information. State requirements may specify the initial collection of information; the method of disclosing information collected before adoption; the updating of existing information; disclosure of updated information; and the maintenance of information in central registries. Tables 21 through 25 provide information on states that have addressed these issues.

Liability for Failure to Comply with Disclosure Requirements

A few states have imposed liability against individuals or agencies that fail to comply with the disclosure requirements contained in state law. Table 26 lists states that have such provisions in law. Other states, as listed in Table 27, expressly limit liability for failure to comply with disclosure requirements.

Summary

State statutes address a range of issues related to the disclosure of nonidentifying information about an adopted child. In considering the requirements under any state's law, an adoption agency should ask the following questions:

- Does the state mandate disclosure of certain health and background information? If not, is disclosure left to the discretion of adoption agencies or the courts?

- When disclosure is mandated, does the requirement apply to all adoptions?

- Who is entitled to disclosure of nonidentifying information? Categories of individuals who may be entitled to this information include adoptive parents, legal guardians, adoptees, descendants of adoptees, the birth family, children who were eligible for adoption but never adopted, and medical personnel.

- Who has the responsibility for collecting nonidentifying information?

- What information must be collected and disclosed? Categories of information may include the child's medical history, other health information about the child, the biological family's medical and genetic history, and the child's and biological family's social and educational history.

- Does state law place a duty to investigate on the adoption agency? If so, what is the scope of that duty?

- Does the state impose specific requirements on the collection and disclosure of information? Requirements may address what type of activity is required in initially collecting information; when this activity should take place; updating of information; disclosure of updated information; and maintenance of information in central registries.

- Does state law impose liability for failure to comply with statutory disclosure requirements? Does state law limit liability for failure to comply with statutory disclosure requirements?

TABLES

Table 1 ◆ **States with Laws Mandating Disclosure of Certain Nonidentifying Information**

State	Statute
Alabama	AL Code §26-10A-31 (Supp. 1991)
Alaska	AK Stat. §18.50.510 (1991)
Arizona	AZ Rev. Stat. Ann. §8-129 (1989)
Arkansas	AR Code Ann. §9-9-505 (Michie 1991)
California	CA Civ. Code §224.70 (West Supp. 1992)
Colorado	CO Rev. Stat. §19-5-207 (Supp. 1990)
Connecticut	CT Gen. Stat. Ann. §45a-746 (West Supp. 1992)
Florida	FL Stat. Ann. §63.162 (West Supp. 1992)
Georgia	GA Code Ann. §19-8-23 (Michie 1991)
Hawaii	HI Rev. Stat. §578.14.5 (Supp. 1991)
Idaho	ID Code §16-1506 (3) (Michie Supp. 1992)
Illinois	IL Ann. Stat. ch. 40, ¶. 1522.4 (Smith-Hurd Supp. 1992)
Indiana	IN Code Ann. §31-3-4-14 (Burns 1987 and Supp. 1991)
Iowa	IA Code Ann. §600.8 (West Supp. 1992)
Kansas	KS Stat. Ann. §59-2130 (Supp. 1991)
Kentucky	KY Rev. Stat. Ann. §199.520 (Michie/Bobbs-Merrill 1991)
Maryland	MD Fam. LAW Code Ann. §5-329.1 (Supp. 1991)
Massachusetts	MA Ann. Laws ch. 210, §5A (Law. Co-op. Supp. 1992)
Michigan	MI. Comp. Laws Ann. §710.68 (West Supp. 1992)
Minnesota	MN Rev. Stat. §259.27 (West Supp. 1992)
Mississippi	MI Code Ann. §93-17-3 (Supp. 1991)
Missouri	MO Ann. Stat. §453.121 (Vernon Supp. 1992)
Montana	MT Code Ann. §40-8-122 (1991)
Nebraska	NE Rev. Stat. §43-107 (Supp. 1990)
New Hampshire	NH Rev. Stat. Ann. §170-B: 19 (1990 and Supp. 1991)
New Jersey	NJ Stat. Ann. §9: 3-41.1 (West Supp. 1992)
New York	NY Soc. Serv. LAW §373-a (McKinney Supp. 1992)
North Carolina	NC Gen. Stat. §48-25 (1991)
North Dakota	ND Cent. Code §14-15-16 (1991)
Ohio	OH Rev. Code Ann. §3107-12 (Anderson 1989)
Oregon	OR Rev. Stat. §109.342 (1991)
Pennsylvania	PA Stat. Ann. tit. 23, §2909 (1991)
South Dakota	SD Codified Laws Ann. §25-6-15.2 (Supp. 1992)
Texas	TX Fam. Code Ann. §16.032 (West Supp. 1992)
Utah	UT Code Ann. §78-30-17 (Supp. 1992)
Vermont	VT Stat. Ann. tit. 15, §461 (1989 and Supp. 1991)
Virginia	VA Code Ann. §63.1-223 (Michie 1992)
Washington	WA Rev. Code Ann. §26.33.350 (West Supp. 1992)
Wisconsin	WI Stat. Ann. §48.432 (West Supp. 1991)
West Virginia	WV Code §48-4-10 (Supp. 1992)
Wyoming	WY Stat. §1-22-116 (1988)

Table 2 ◆ **States That Give Agencies Discretion Regarding Disclosure of Nonidentifying Information**

State	Statute	Who has discretion to decide whether to disclose
Delaware	DE Code Ann. tit. 13, §924 (Supp. 1990)	Gives public or private adoption agencies discretion to release nonidentifying information; court order may require release of health-related information when agency refuses to release.
Oklahoma	OK Stat. Ann. tit. 10, §57 (West Supp. 1992)	Gives authority to release medical information to Department of Human Services, any certified adoption agency, or any licensed child-placing agency with custody of a child available for adoption.
South Carolina	SC Code Ann. §20-7-1780 (Law. Co-op. Supp. 1991)	Sole discretion given to chief executive officer (CEO) of adoption agency if CEO perceives release would "serve the best interests of the persons concerned."

Table 3   ◆ States That Give Courts Discretion Regarding Disclosure of Nonidentifying Information

State	Statute	Provision for court discretion re: decision to release information
District of Columbia	DC Code Ann. §16-311 (1989)	Order of court required; order permitted but only "when the court is satisfied that the welfare of the child will thereby be promoted or protected."
Louisiana	LA Stat. Ann. CH.C. Art. 1188 (West 1991)	Court order is "exclusive means for gaining access" to information.
Maine	ME Rev. Stat. Ann. tit. 19, §534 (West Supp. 1991)	"Adoption records may be examined only upon authorization by the judge of the probate court."
Nevada	NV Rev. Stat. §127.140 (1985)	Information is not to be disclosed "except upon an order of the court expressly so permitting."
New Mexico	NM Stat. Ann. §40-7-53 (Michie 1989)	Inspection of social and medical records only "upon application to the clerk of the court."
Rhode Island	RI Gen. Laws §8-10-3 (Supp. 1991)	Statute places authority with family court.
Tennessee	TN Code Ann. §36-1-131 (Michie 1991)	Judge or chancellor may issue an order to "open the record if in the opinion of the judge or chancellor, it is in the best interest of the child or public to have such information disclosed."

Table 4 ◆ **States That Limit Disclosure Requirements to Agency Adoptions**

State	Statute	Provision
California	CA Civ. Code §224.70 (West Supp. 1992)	References the department or delegated county adoption agency.
Georgia	GA Code Ann. §19-8-23 (Michie 1991)	References adoptions by the department and child-placing agencies.
Illinois	IL Ann. Stat. ch. 40, ¶1522.4 (Smith-Hurd Supp. 1992)	References agencies, the Department of Children and Family Services, and court services divisions.
New Jersey	NJ Stat. Ann. §9: 3-41 (West Supp. 1992)	References "approved agencies."
New York	NY Soc. Serv. Law §373-9 (McKinney Supp. 1992)	References "authorized agencies."
Oklahoma	OK Stat. Ann. tit. 10, §57 (West Supp. 1992)	References the Department of Human Services, certified adoption agencies, and licensed child-placing agencies.
South Carolina	SC Code Ann. §20-7-1780 (Law. Co-op. Supp. 1991)	References adoption proceedings in the State Department of Social Services or in any authorized agency.

Table 5 ◆ **States That Exclude Stepparent or Relative Adoptions from Disclosure Requirements**

State	Statute	Provision
Montana	MT Code Ann. §40-8-122 (1991)	Duty to obtain information may be waived by the court or the department if the petitioner is a stepparent or a member of the child's extended family.
Nebraska	NE Rev. Stat. §43-107 (1988)	Adoption of children by stepparents is exempted from investigation and disclosure requirements.
Oregon	OR Rev. Stat. §109.342(5) (1991)	Requirement to obtain a medical history does not apply when a person is adopted by a stepparent.
Texas	TX Fam. Code Ann. §16.032 (West Supp. 1992)	Report on child's history and disclosure not required for adoptions by the child's stepparent, grandparent, or aunt or uncle by birth, marriage or prior adoption.

Table 6 ◆ **States That Permit Disclosure to Adoptive and Prospective Adoptive Parents When Information Is Sought**

State	Statute	Provision
Delaware	DE Code Ann. tit. 13, §924 (Supp. 1990)	Agency has discretion to release information "to any parties to the adoption."
Minnesota	MN Stat. Ann. §259.27 (West Supp. 1992)	Statute specifically authorizes report to prospective adoptive parents.
Mississippi	MS Code Ann. §93-17-3 (Supp. 1991)	Any information in doctor's certificate that indicates "any abnormal mental or physical condition or defect" must be communicated to "adopting parents" who must file "an affidavit stating full and complete knowledge of such condition or defect."
New Mexico	NM Stat. Ann. §40-7-53 (Michie 1989)	Inspection of records containing information by biological parent or adoptee is permitted.
South Carolina	SC Code Ann. §20-7-1780 (Law. Co-op. Supp. 1991)	At discretion of agency chief executive officer, nonidentifying information may be disclosed to adoptive parents.
Tennessee	TN Code Ann. §36-1-131 (1991)	At discretion of court, information may be released "to the party requiring it."
West Virginia	WV Code §48-4-10 (1986 and Supp. 1992)	Information shall be provided to adoptive parents as guardians of the adopted child.

Table 7 ◆ States That Permit Disclosure to Legal Guardians When Information Is Sought

State	Statute	Provision
Arizona	AZ Rev. Stat. Ann. §8-129 (1989)	Permits disclosure to child's guardian if adoptive parents have died.
Arkansas	AK Code Ann. §9-9-505 (Michie 1991)	Permits disclosure to child's guardian if adoptive parents have died.
Maine	ME Rev. Stat. Ann. tit. 19, §534 (West Supp. 1991)	Disclosure to be made to "adoptive parents or legal guardian on petition to the court."
Missouri	MO Ann. Stat. §453.121 (Vernon Supp. 1992)	Disclosure may be made to adoptive parents or legal guardians.
Texas	TX Fam. Code Ann. §16.032 (West Supp. 1992)	Disclosure may be made to adoptive parents or "the managing conservator, guardian of the person, or legal custodian of the adopted child."
Utah	UT Code Ann. §78-30-17 (Supp. 1992)	Disclosure may be made to the "adoptee's legal guardian" in the event of adoptive parents' death.
Wisconsin	WI Stat. Ann. §48.432 (West Supp. 1991)	Disclosure may be made to an adoptive parent or "the guardian or legal custodian of an individual or adoptee."

Table 8 ◆ States That Mandate Disclosure of Some Nonidentifying Information to Adopted Persons

State	Statute	Age at Which Adoptee Is Entitled to Disclosure
Alabama	AL Code §26-10A-31 (Supp. 1991)	19 or older
Alaska	AK Stat. §18.50.500 (1991)	18 or older
Arizona	AZ Rev. Stat. Ann. §8-129 (1989)	18 or older
Arkansas	AR Code Ann. §9-9-505 (Michie 1991)	18 or older
California	CA Civ. Code §224.73 (West Supp. 1992)	21 or older
Connecticut	CT Gen. Stat. Ann. §45a-746 (West Supp. 1992)	adult
Florida	FL Stat. Ann. §63.162 (West Supp. 1992)	18 or older
Georgia	GA Code Ann. §19-8-23 (Michie 1991)	21 or older
Hawaii	HI Rev. Stat. §578-14.5 (Supp. 1991)	upon majority
Illinois	IL Ann. Stat. ch. 40, ¶1522.4 (Smith-Hurd Supp. 1992)	18 or older
Indiana	IN Code Ann. §31-3-4-14 (Burn's 1987 and Supp. 1991)	no restriction
Iowa	IA Code Ann. §600.16 (West Supp. 1992)	adult
Kansas	KS Stat. Ann. §59-2122 (Supp. 1991)	adult
Kentucky	KY Rev. Stat. Ann. §199.520 (Michie/ Bobbs-Merrill 1991)	adult
Louisiana	LA Rev. Stat. Ch. C. Art. 1188 (West 1991)	no restriction
Massachusetts	MA Gen. Laws Ann. ch. 210, §5D (Law Co-op. Supp. 1992)	18 or older
Michigan	MI Comp. Laws Ann. §710.68(7) (West Supp. 1992)	adult
Minnesota	MN Stat. Ann. §259.47 (West Supp. 1992)	19 or older is implied
Missouri	MO Ann. Stat. §453.121 (Vernon Supp. 1992)	21 or older
Nebraska	NE Rev. Stat. §43-146.02 (1988)	no restriction

Table 8 ♦ (continued)

State	Statute	Age at Which Adoptee Is Entitled to Disclosure
New Hampshire	NH Rev. Stat. Ann. §170-B:19 (1990 and Supp. 1991)	21 or older
New Mexico	NM Stat. Ann. §40-7-53 (Michie 1989)	18 or older
New York	NY Soc. Serv. Law §373-9 (McKinney Supp. 1992)	adopted former foster child and youth when discharged from foster care to own care
North Carolina	NC Gen. Stat. §48-25(e) (1991)	21 or older
North Dakota	ND Cent. Code §14-15-16 (1991)	adult
Ohio	OH Rev. Code Ann. §3107.17 (Anderson 1989)	age of majority
Oregon	OR Rev. Stat. §109.342 (1991)	age of majority
South Dakota	SD Codified Laws Ann. §25-6-15.2 (Supp. 1992)	18 or older
Texas	TX Fam. Code Ann. §16.032(2)(i)(3) (West Supp. 1992)	adult
Utah	UT Code Ann. §78-30-17 (1992)	no restriction
Vermont	VT Stat. Ann. tit. 15, §461(a) (1989)	no restriction
Wisconsin	WI Stat. Ann. §48.432(3)(a)(1) (West Supp. 1991)	18 or older
Wyoming	WY Stat. §1-22-116 (1988)	age of majority

Table 9 ◆ **States That Permit Disclosure of Nonidentifying Information to Adopted Persons at Agency or Court Discretion**

State	Statute	Age at Which Adoptee Is Entitled to Disclosure
Maine	ME Rev. Stat. Ann. tit. 19 §534 (West Supp. 1991)	18 or older
Maryland	MD Fam. LAW Code Ann. §5-329(a) (Supp. 1991)	no restriction
Pennsylvania	PA Stat. Ann. tit. 23, §2905 (1991)	18 or older
South Carolina	SC Code Ann. §20-7-1780(D) (Law. Co-op. Supp. 1991)	no restriction
Tennessee	TN Code Ann. §36-1-131(a) (1991)	no restriction
Washington	WA Rev. Code Ann. §26.33.340 (West Supp. 1992)	no restriction
West Virginia	WV Code §48-4-10(a) (1986 and Supp. 1992)	adult

Table 10 ◆ **States with No Specific Provision for Disclosure of Nonidentifying Information to Adopted Persons** (as of September 1992)

Colorado	Nevada
Delaware	New Jersey
District of Columbia	Oklahoma
Idaho	Rhode Island
Mississippi	Virginia
Montana	

Table 11 ◆ **States That Permit Disclosure of Nonidentifying Information to Individuals Other than Adoptive Parents, Legal Guardians, and Adopted Persons**

1. Descendants of Adoptees

State	Statute	Eligible Individuals
Arizona	AZ Rev. Stat. Ann. §8-129(B) (3)(d) (1989)	Any descendant after death of adoptee.
California	CA Civ. Code §1789.24(s) (West 1985 and Supp. 1992)	Any child or grandchild; no requirement of death of adoptee (disclosure limited to medically necessary information).
Connecticut	CT Gen. Stat. Ann. §45a-746 (West Supp. 1992)	Adult descendants after death of adoptee.
Maine	ME Rev. Stat. Ann. tit. 19, §534 (West 1981 and Supp. 1991)	All descendants upon petition to court; no requirement of death of adoptee.
Oregon	OR Rev. Stat. §109.500(1)(d)(B) (1991)	Any descendant of adoptee 18 years of age or older upon death of adoptee.
Texas	TX Fam. Code Ann. §16.032(i)(5) (West Supp. 1992)	Adult descendants after death of adoptee.
Utah	UT Code Ann. §78-30-17(4)(e) (1992)	Any child or descendant of adoptee, no age restriction.
Wisconsin	WI Stat. Ann. §48.432(3) (West Supp. 1991)	Descendants age 18 or older of adoptee; no requirement of adoptee's death.

Table 11 ◆ (continued)

2. Birth Family

State	Statute	Eligible Individuals
Alabama	AL Code §26-10A-31(g)(2) (Supp. 1991)	Biological parents.
Arizona	AZ Rev. Stat. Ann. §8-129(3)(e) (1989)	Biological parents; other biological children of the biological parents.
Arkansas	AR Code Ann. §9-9-505(b)(2)(D) (Michie 1991)	Biological parents.
Colorado	CO Rev. Stat. §19-5-207(3) (Supp. 1991)	Biological parents.
Indiana	IN Code Ann. §31-3-4-6(2),-6(4),-14(a)(1) (Burns 1987 and Supp. 1991)	Biological parents; relatives of biological parents.
Massachusetts	MA Ann. Laws ch. 210, §5D(2) (Law. Co-op. 1981 and Supp. 1992)	Biological parents.
Michigan	MI Comp. Laws Ann. §710.68a(2) (West Supp. 1992)	Biological parents; adult biological siblings of adoptee.
Minnesota	MN Stat. Ann. §259.47(1) (West 1982 and Supp. 1992)	Biological parents.
Oregon	OR Rev. Stat. §109.500(1)(b) (1991)	Biological parents.
Utah	UT Code Ann. §78-30-17(4)(f)-(g) (1992)	Biological parents; adult siblings of adoptee.
Washington	WA Rev. Code Ann. §26.33.340 (West 1986 and Supp. 1992)	Biological parents.

Table 11 ◆ (continued)

3. ChildrenWhose Parents' Rights Were Termininated but Who Were Not Adopted

State	Statute	Eligible Individuals
Connecticut	CT Gen. Stat. Ann. §45a-746(4) (West Supp. 1992)	"Adult adoptable persons" and their adult descendants after death of adoptee; both parents' rights must have been terminated.

4. Medical Personnel

State	Statute	Eligible Individuals
Georgia	GA Code Ann. §19-8-23(d) (Michie Supp. 1992)	A provider of medical services may petition the court to release medical information to providers of medical services.
Iowa	IA Code Ann. §600.16(1)(c) (West 1981 and Supp. 1992)	Person approved by the department of social services may obtain medical history in order to treat individual in a medical facility.
Nebraska	NE Rev. Stat. §43-146.03 (1988)	Court may approve release of birth certificate information upon request of physician or psychologist if information is necessary for treatment.

Table 12 ◆ Who Has Responsibility for Collecting Nonidentifying Information?

State	Statute	Requirement
Alabama	AL Code §26-10A-19 (Supp. 1991)	State agency or licensed child-placing agency when requested by individual or couple seeking to adopt; agency or individual appointed by the court.
Alaska	AK Stat. §25.23.185 (1991)	Agency or individual who places the child for adoption or petitioner.
Arizona	AZ Rev. Stat. Ann §8-129 (1989)	Division, agency, or individual who places the child.
Arkansas	AR Code Ann. §9-9-505 (Michie 1991)	Licensed adoption agency or person, entity, or organization handling the adoption.
California	CA Civ. Code §222.26 (West Supp. 1992)	Agency placing the child for adoption.
Colorado	CO Rev. Stat. §19-5-207 (Supp. 1990)	County department of social services, licensed child-placing agency, or individual placing child for adoption.
Connecticut	CT Gen. Stat. Ann. §45a-748 (West Supp. 1992)	Agency or department making the placement.
Delaware	DE Code Ann. tit. 13 §912(a) (Supp. 1990)	Department or authorized agency upon order of court.
District of Columbia	DC Code Ann. §16-307 (1989)	Licensed child-placing agency or mayor upon court referral.
Florida	FL Stat. Ann. §63.162 (West Supp. 1992)	State department or agency.
Georgia	GA Code Ann. §19-8-16 (Michie Supp. 1992)	"Child-placing agency appointed by the court or any other independent agent appointed by the court."
Hawaii	HI Rev. Stat. §578.14.5 (Supp. 1991)	Public agencies and child-placing agencies approved by the department of human services.
Idaho	ID Rev. Stat. §16-1506(3) (Michie Supp. 1992)	As ordered by court.

Table 12 ✦ (continued)

State	Statute	Requirement
Illinois	IL Ann. Stat. ch. 40, ¶1522.4 (Smith-Hurd Supp. 1992)	Agency, the department, or court services units.
Indiana	IN Code Ann. §31-8-1-2 (Burns, 1987 and Supp. 1991)	Petitioner for adoption.
Iowa	IA Code Ann. §600.8 (West Supp. 1992)	"Person making the investigation."
Kansas	KS Stat. Ann. §59-2128 (Supp. 1991)	Petitioner for adoption.
Kentucky	KY Rev. Stat. Ann. §199.520 (Michie/Bobbs-Merrill 1991)	The department or the agency making placement.
Louisiana	LA Rev. Stat. Ch. C. Art. 1173 (West 1991)	As determined by the department of social services.
Maine	ME Rev. Stat. Ann. tit. 19, §533 (West Supp. 1991)	The department.
Maryland	MD Fam. LAW Code Ann. §5-328 (Supp. 1991)	"The person authorized to place a minor child for adoption."
Massachusetts	MA Ann. Laws ch. 210, §5A (Law. Co-op. Supp. 1992)	Department of social services.
Michigan	MI Comp. Laws Ann. §710.27 (West Supp. 1992)	The child-placing agency, the department, or the court.
Minnesota	MN Stat. Ann. §259-47 (West Supp. 1992)	The agency responsible for the placement.
Mississippi	MS Code Ann. §93-17-3 (Supp. 1991)	Petitioner for adoption.
Missouri	MO Ann. Stat. §453.121 (Vernon Supp. 1992)	Child-placing agency or juvenile court.

Table 12 ◆ (continued)

State	Statute	Requirement
Montana	MT Code Ann. §40-8-121 (1991)	Upon order of the court: the department, a licensing child-placing agency, or other person.
Nebraska	NE Rev. Stat. §43-107 (Supp. 1990)	Upon court order: the department of social services or a licensed child placement agency.
New Hampshire	NH Rev. Stat. Ann. (1990 and Supp. 1991)	Responsibility not specified.
New Jersey	NJ Stat. Ann. §9:3-41.1 (West Supp. 1992)	"Any approved agency making an investigation of the facts and circumstances surrounding the surrender of a child."
New Mexico	NM Stat. Ann. §40-7-53 (Michie 1989)	Responsibility not specified.
New York	NY Soc. Serv. Law §373-a (McKinney Supp. 1992)	An authorized agency.
Nevada	NV Rev. Stat. §127.120(1) (1985)	The welfare division of the department of human resources.
North Carolina	NC Gen. Stat. §48-25 (1991)	County department of social services or licensed child-placing agency.
North Dakota	ND Cent. Code §14-15-16 (1991)	Department of human services.
Ohio	OH Rev. Code Ann. §3107-12 (Anderson 1989)	Department of human services, an agency, or other person appointed by the court.
Oklahoma	OK Stat. Ann. tit. 10, §57(C) (West Supp. 1992)	Department of human services, any certified adoption agency, or any licensed child-placing agency having custody of the child.
Oregon	OR Rev. Stat. §109.342 (1991)	Responsibility not specified.
Pennsylvania	PA Stat. Ann. tit. 23, §2909 (1991)	Intermediary to deliver information to the adopting parents or their physician.

Table 12 ◆ (continued)

State	Statute	Requirement
Rhode Island	RI Gen. Laws §8-10-3 (Supp. 1991)	Responsibility not specified.
South Carolina	SC Code Ann. §20-7-1780 (Law. Co-op. Supp. 1991)	Chief executive officer of the agency.
South Dakota	SD Codified Laws Ann. §25-6-15.2 (Supp. 1992)	Department of social services.
Tennessee	TN Code Ann. §36-1-131 (Michie 1991)	The court.
Texas	TX Fam. Code Ann. §16-032 (West Supp. 1992)	Texas Department of Human Services, an authorized agency, or the child's parent or guardian.
Utah	UT Code Ann. §78-30-17 (Supp. 1992)	Person who proceeded on behalf of the petitioner for adoption or a licensed child-placing agency if involved.
Vermont	VT Stat. Ann. tit. 15, §436 (1989)	Parent who surrenders child for adoption.
Virginia	VA Code Ann. §63.1-223 (Michie 1992)	Public welfare department or licensed child-placing agency.
Washington	WA Rev. Code Ann. §26.33.350 (West Supp. 1992)	"Every person, firm, society, association, or corporation receiving, securing a home for, or otherwise caring for a minor child."
West Virginia	WV Code Ann. §48-4-10 (Supp. 1992)	Clerk of the court.
Wisconsin	WI Stat. Ann. §48.432(3) (West Supp. 1991)	The department.
Wyoming	WY Stat. §1-22-116	An authorized agency or by order of the court.

Table 13 ◆ States That Require Collection and Disclosure of the Child's Medical History

State	Requirement
Alabama	"Health and medical history of adoptee."
Arkansas	"Health history" of child.
California	"Medical report on the child's medical background."
Colorado	"Physical and mental condition of the child."
Illinois	"Medical and health histories of a child legally freed for adoption."
Indiana	"A medical report of the health status and medical history of the adoptee."
Iowa	A "complete medical and developmental history of the person to be adopted."
Kansas	"A complete written genetic, medical, and social history of the child."
Michigan	"Medical history of the adoptee."
Minnesota	No statutory requirement, but Minnesota Rules require that a written health history of the child be shared with adoptive parents. Minn. R. 9560.0060 (1991)
Nebraska	"The available medical history of the person placed for adoption."
New Jersey	The child's "developmental and medical history."
New York	"Medical histories of a child legally freed for adoption."
Ohio	"The physical, mental, and developmental condition of the minor."
Oklahoma	"The medical history of the child to be adopted."
Oregon	"A medical history of the child."
South Carolina	"The health and medical history of the adoptee."
Texas	"The available health, social, educational, and genetic history of the child to be adopted."
Utah	Adoptee's "health history."
Virginia	"Physical and mental condition of the child."
Washington	"A complete medical report containing all available information concerning the mental, physical, and sensory handicaps of the child."
Wyoming	"The medical history of the child."

Table 14 ◆ **States That Do Not Specifically Require Collection and Disclosure of the Child's Medical History**
(as of September 1992)

Alaska	Missouri
Arizona	Mississippi
Colorado	Montana
Delaware	New Hampshire
District of Columbia	Nebraska
Florida	North Carolina
Georgia	North Dakota
Hawaii	Pennsylvania
Idaho	Rhode Island
Kentucky	South Dakota
Louisiana	Tennessee
Maine	Vermont
Maryland	West Virginia
Massachusetts	Wisconsin

Table 15 ◆ States That Require the Inclusion of Specific Information in the Child's Medical History

Prenatal and Neonatal Information	Child's Medical Problems	Child's Developmental History	Child's Psychological and/or Psychiatric History
Illinois: "Drugs or medication taken by the child's biological mother during pregnancy."	Oklahoma: "Diseases, illnesses, accidents, allergies and congenital defects."	California: "Developmental history and family life."	California: "Psychological evaluations."
New Jersey: "Any drugs or medications taken during pregnancy."	Oregon: "Disease, disability, congenital or birth defects."	Iowa: "Complete developmental history."	Illinois: "Psychological and psychiatric information."
New York: "Any drugs or medication taken during pregnancy by the child's natural mother."	Washington: "The child's x-rays, examinations, hospitalizations, and immunizations."	New Jersey: "Information relevant to the child's development, including... personality and temperament."	New York: "Any psychological information" on child.
Oklahoma: "Drugs taken and consumption of alcohol during the pregnancy of the mother."			Oklahoma: "Psychological evaluations."
Oregon: "A gynecological and obstetrical history of the biological mother."			Texas: "History must include... psychological [and] psychiatric... history."
Texas: "History must include birth, neonatal, and other medical...results."			Utah: The adoptee's "medical history, including...psychological evaluations."
Utah: The adoptee's "medical history, including neonatal...history."			Washington: "A complete medical report...concerning the mental... handicaps of the child."
Wyoming: "Any drugs or medication taken during pregnancy by the child's natural mother."			

Table 16 ◆ **Collection and Disclosure of Medical and Genetic History**

State	Collect and Disclose the Medical History of the Birth Parents	Collect and Disclose the Medical History of Other Relatives	Collect and Disclose Genetic History
Alabama	AL Code §26-10A-19 (Supp. 1991)	No	No
Alaska	AK Stat. §18.50.510 (1991)	AK Stat. §18.50.510 (1991)	No
Arizona	AZ Rev. Stat. Ann. §8-129 (1989)	AZ Rev. Stat. Ann. §8-129 (1989)	AZ Rev. Stat. Ann. §8-129 (1989)
Arkansas	AR Code Ann. §§9-9-505, -506 (Michie 1991)	AR Code Ann. §9-9-505 (Michie 1991)	AR Code Ann. §§9-9-505, -506 (Michie 1991)
California	CA Civ. Code §224.70(a) (West Supp. 1992)	No	CA Civ. Code §224.70(b) (West Supp. 1992)
Colorado	No	No	No
Connecticut	CT Gen. Stat. Ann. §45a-746 (West Supp. 1992)	CT Gen. Stat. Ann. §45a-746 (West Supp. 1992)	No
Delaware	No	No	No
District of Columbia	No	No	No
Florida	No	No	No
Georgia	No	No	No
Hawaii	HI Rev. Stat. §578.14.5 (Supp. 1991)	HI Rev. Stat. §578.14.5 (Supp. 1991)	HI Rev. Stat. §578.14.5 (Supp. 1991)
Idaho	ID Code §16-1506 (Supp. 1992)	No	ID Code §16-1506 (Supp. 1992)

Table 16 ◆ (continued)

State	Collect and Disclose the Medical History of the Birth Parents	Collect and Disclose the Medical History of Other Relatives	Collect and Disclose Genetic History
Illinois	IL Ann. Stat. ch. 40 ¶1522.4 (Smith-Hurd Supp. 1992)	IL Ann. Stat. ch. 40 ¶1522.4 (Smith-Hurd Supp. 1992)	IL Ann. Stat. ch. 40 ¶1522.4 (Smith-Hurd Supp. 1992)
Indiana	IN Code Ann. §§31-3-1-2 (Burns 1987 and Supp. 1991)	No	No
Iowa	IA Code Ann. §600.8 (West Supp. 1992)	IA Code Ann. §600.8 (West Supp. 1992)	IA Code Ann. §600.8 (West Supp. 1992)
Kansas	KS Stat. Ann. §59-2130 (Supp. 1991)	No	KS Stat. Ann. §59-2130 (Supp. 1991)
Kentucky	KY Rev. Stat. Ann. §199.520 (Michie/Bobbs-Merrill 1991)	KY Rev. Stat. Ann. §199.520 (Michie/Bobbs-Merrill 1991)	No
Louisiana	No	No	No
Maine	No	No	No
Maryland	MD Fam. Law Code Ann. §5-328 (Supp. 1991)	No	No
Massachusetts	No	No	No
Michigan	MI Comp. Laws Ann. §710.27 (West Supp. 1992)	MI Comp. Laws Ann. §710.27 (West Supp. 1992)	No
Minnesota	MN Stat. Ann. §§259.46-.49 (West 1982 & Supp. 1992)	No	MN Stat. Ann. §§259.46-49 (West 1982 & Supp. 1992)

Table 16   ◆ (continued)

State	Collect and Disclose the Medical History of the Birth Parents	Collect and Disclose the Medical History of Other Relatives	Collect and Disclose Genetic History
Mississippi	No	No	No
Missouri	MO Ann. Stat. §453.121 (Vernon Supp. 1992)	MO Ann. Stat. §453.121 (Vernon Supp. 1992)	No
Montana	MT Code Ann. §40-8-122 (1991)	No	No
Nebraska	NE Rev. Stat. §43-107 (1988)	NE Rev. Stat. §43-107 (1988)	No
New Hampshire	NH Rev. Stat. Ann. §170-B:19 (1990 & Supp. 1991)	NH Rev. Stat. Ann. §170-B:19 (1990 & Supp. 1991)	No
New Jersey	NJ Stat. Ann. §9.3-41.1 (West Supp. 1992)	No	NJ Stat. Ann. §9.3-41.1 (West Supp. 1992)
New Mexico	NM Stat. Ann. §40-7-53 (Michie 1989)	No	No
New York	NY Soc. Serv. Law §373-a (McKinney Supp. 1992)	No	NY Soc. Serv. LAW §373-a (McKinney Supp. 1992)
Nevada	No	No	No
North Carolina	NC Gen. Stat. §48-25 (1991)	NC Gen. Stat. §48-25 (1991)	No
North Dakota	No	No	No
Ohio	OH Rev. Code Ann. §3107.12 (Anderson 1989)	No	OH Rev. Code Ann. §3107.12 (Anderson 1989)

Table 16 ◆ (continued)

State	Collect and Disclose the Medical History of the Birth Parents	Collect and Disclose the Medical History of Other Relatives	Collect and Disclose Genetic History
Oklahoma	OK Stat. Ann. tit. 10, §60.5A (West 1987 & Supp. 1992)	OK Stat. Ann. tit. 10, §60.5A (West 1987 & Supp. 1992)	No
Oregon	OR Rev. Stat. §109.342 (2)(a)(1991)	No	OR Rev. Stat. §109.342 (2)(a)(1991) (both parents)
Pennsylvania	No	No	No
Rhode Island	No	No	No
South Carolina	SC Code Ann. §20.7-1740 (Law. Co-op Supp. 1991)	SC Code Ann. §20.7-1740 (Law. Co-op Supp. 1991)	SC Code Ann. §20.7-1740 (Law. Co-op Supp. 1991)
South Dakota	SD Codified Laws Ann. §25-6-15.2 (Supp. 1991)	SD Codified Laws Ann. §25-6-15.2 (Supp. 1991)	No
Tennessee	No	No	No
Texas	TX Fam. Code. Ann. §16.032 (West Supp. 1992)	TX Fam. Code. Ann. §16.032 (West Supp. 1992)	TX Fam. Code. Ann. §16.032 (West Supp. 1992)
Utah	UT Code Ann. §78-30-16 (1992)	UT Code Ann. §78-30-16 (1992)	UT Code Ann. §§78-30-16, -17 (1992)
Vermont	VT Stat. Ann. tit. 15, §§436(c), 460, 461 (1989 & Supp. 1991)	No	No
Virginia	VA Code. Ann. §63.1-223 (Michie 1992)	No	No

Table 16 ✦ (continued)

State	Collect and Disclose the Medical History of the Birth Parents	Collect and Disclose the Medical History of Other Relatives	Collect and Disclose Genetic History
Washington	WA Rev. Code Ann. §26.33.350 (West Supp. 1992)	WA Rev. Code Ann. §26.33.350 (West Supp. 1992)	No
West Virginia	No	No	No
Wisconsin	WI Stat. Ann. §48.432 (West Supp. 1991)	WI Stat. Ann. §48.432 (West Supp. 1991)	WI Stat. Ann. §48.432 (West Supp. 1991)
Wyoming	WY Stat. §1-22-203 (1988 & Supp. 1991)	No	WY Stat. §1-22-203 (1988 & Supp. 1991)

Table 17 ◆ States That Require Disclosure of the Child's Social and Educational History

Social History

State	Statute
Alabama	AL Code §26-10A-31 (Supp. 1991)
California	CA Civ. Code §224-70(a) (West Supp. 1992)
Florida	FL Stat. Ann. §63.082 (West 1985 and Supp. 1992)
Kansas	KS Stat. Ann. §59-2130 (Supp. 1991)
Massachusetts	MA Ann. Laws ch. 210, §50 (Law. Co-op. Supp. 1992)
New Mexico	NM Stat. Ann. §40-7-53 (Michie 1989)
Tennessee	TN Code Ann. §36-1-114 (1991)
Texas	TX Fam. Code Ann. §16.032 (West Supp. 1992)
Utah	UT Code Ann. §78-30-16 (1992)
Washington	WA Rev. Code Ann. §26.33.380 (West Supp. 1992)
Wisconsin	WI Stat. Ann. §48.432 (West Supp. 1991)

Educational History

State	Statute
California	CA Civ. Code §224.70(a) (West Supp. 1992)
Massachusetts	MA Ann. Laws ch. 210, §5A (Law. Co-op. 1981)
Texas	TX Fam. Code Ann. §16.032 (West Supp. 1992)

Table 18 ◆ States That Require Disclosure of Biological Parents' Social History

State	Statute
Alaska	AK Stat. §18.50.510 (1991)
Connecticut	CT Gen. Stat. Ann. §47a-746 (West Supp. 1992)
Kansas	KS Stat. Ann. §59-2130 Supp. 1991)
Illinois	IL Ann. Stat. ch. 40, ¶1522.4 (Smith-Hurd Supp. 1992)
New Mexico	NM Stat. Ann. §40-7-53(D) (Michie 1989)
Ohio	OH Rev. Code Ann. §3107.12 (D)(3) (Anderson 1989)
South Dakota	SD Codified Laws Ann. §25-6-15.2 (Supp. 1992)
Texas	TX Fam. Code Ann. §16.032 (West Supp. 1992)
Vermont	VT Stat. Ann. tit. 15, §436(c) (1989)
Washington	WA Rev. Code Ann. §26.33.380 (West Supp. 1992)

Table 19 ◆ States That Place the Duty to Investigate with Adoption Agencies

State	Statute	*Extent of the Agency's Duty to Investigate*
Arizona	AZ Rev. Stat. Ann. §8-129(A) (1989)	Compile and provide "reasonably available" information.
Connecticut	CT Gen. Stat. Ann. §45a-748 (West Supp. 1992)	Make "reasonable efforts" to obtain information.
Hawaii	HI Rev. Stat. §578-14.5(b) (Supp. 1991)	Make "reasonable efforts" to obtain information.
Idaho	ID Code §16-1506(3) (Supp. 1992)	Include "reasonably known or available" medical and genetic information.
New Jersey	NJ Stat. Ann. §9:3-41.1 (West Supp. 1992)	Supply all "available" information.
New York	NY Soc. Serv. Law §373-a (McKinney Supp. 1992)	Provide information "to the extent [it] is available."
Ohio	OH Rev. Code Ann. §3107.12 (Anderson 1989)	Specifies in detail procedures to be utilized in obtaining medical and social history.
Wyoming	WY Stat. §1-22-116 (1988 and Supp. 1992)	Provide information "to the extent available."

Table 20 ◆ **States That Place the Duty to Investigate with Non-Agency Entities**

State	Statute	Requirement
Florida	FL Stat. Ann. §63.082 (West 1985 and Supp. 1992)	Duty placed on parent who relinquishes child: Department "shall provide a consent form and a family history form to an intermediary who intends to place a child for adoption. Said forms completed by the natural parent or parents shall be attached to the petition and shall contain such biological or sociological information, or such information as to the family medical history."
Iowa	IA Code Ann. §600.8(4) (West 1981 and Supp. 1992)	Any person with relevant background information about a child to be adopted shall cooperate with the investigator upon request.
Oklahoma	OK Stat. Ann. tit. 10, §60.5A (West 1987)	Duty placed on parent who relinquishes a child: "parent shall complete a medical history form...containing, as far as is ascertainable," the medical histories of child and birth family.

Table 21 ◆ States with Statutes That Address the Initial Collection of Nonidentifying Information

State	Statute	Required Activity Regarding Collection of Information	When Required
Arizona	AZ Rev. Stat. Ann. §8-129(A) (1989)	Provide prospective parents with specific documents containing health and genetic history.	Prior to adoption.
Arkansas	AR Code Ann. §9-9-505(a) (Michie 1991)	Provide adoptive parent(s) with detailed written health, genetic, and social information.	Prior to placement for adoption.
California	CA Civ. Code §§222.26, 224.70 (West Supp. 1992)	Provide adoptive parent(s) with written medical report of the child's medical background.	Prior to placement or, if private adoption, as part of home study.
Colorado	CO Rev. Stat. §19-5-207(2) (1990 and Supp. 1991)	Agency to prepare a written report of medical and social information (to be attached to petition for adoption).	Prior to filing adoption petition.
Connecticut	CT Gen. Stat. Ann. §45a-746 (West Supp. 1992)	Agency to prepare information "in writing on a form provided by the department."	Not later than date of finalizing adoption.
Kentucky	KY Rev. Stat. Ann. §199.520(4)(a) (Michie/Bobbs Merrill 1991)	Information to be "in writing, on a standardized form."	Not later than date of finalizing adoption.
Louisiana	LA Rev. Stat. Ch.C. Art. 1173 (West 1991)	Department of social services to promulgate rules and regulations.	Department of social services to promulgate rules and regulations.

Table 21   ◆ (continued)

State	Statute	Required Activity Regarding Collection of Information	When Required
Mississippi	MI Code Ann. §93-17-3 (Supp.1991)	Preparation of a doctor's certificate showing child's condition.	Prior to filing adoption petition.
North Carolina	NC Gen. Stat. §48-25(e) (1991)	Agency shall "give" a complete health history to adoptive parent(s).	Not later than date of finalizing adoption.
Ohio	OH Rev. Code Ann. §3107.12(D)(3) (Anderson 1989)	Obtain information through interviews with biological parents or other persons and through review of available records.	File with court at least 10 days before petition for adoption is heard.
Oklahoma	OK Stat. Ann. tit. 10, §60.5A (West 1987 and Supp. 1992)	Complete "a medical history form."	When consent to adoption is given, or filed with petition for consent of court.
Oregon	OR Rev. Stat. §109.342(1), (6) (1991)	Department to "prescribe a form for compilation of the medical history," to be given to prospective adoptive parent(s).	Not later than date of finalizing adoption.
Texas	TX Fam. Code Ann. §16.032(a) (West Supp. 1992)	Agency "shall compile a report."	Prior to adoptive placement of child.
Washington	WA Rev. Code Ann. §26.33.350 (West Supp. 1992)	Any entity "caring for a minor" shall "make available ...a complete medical report."	Prior to placement.

Table 22 ◆ **States with Statutes That Require Disclosure of Information Collected Prior to Adoption**

State	Statute	When Required
Alabama	AL Code §26-10A-19 (Supp. 1991)	Prior to or upon issuance of final decree of adoption.
Alaska	AK Stat. §18.50.510 (1986)	Prior to or upon issuance of final decree of adoption.
Arizona	AZ Rev. Stat. Ann. §8-129(A) (1989)	Prior to adoptive placement.
Connecticut	CT Gen. Stat. Ann. §45a-746 (West Supp. 1992)	Prior to or upon issuance of final decree of adoption.
Florida	FL Stat. Ann. §63-162(f) (West Supp. 1992)	Prior to or upon issuance of final decree of adoption.
Hawaii	HI Rev. Stat. §578.14.5(c) (Supp. 1991)	Prior to or upon filing the petition for adoption.
Illinois	IL Ann. Stat. ch. 40, ¶1522.4 (Smith-Hurd Supp. 1992)	Not later than the date of placement with the petitioning adoptive parent.
Kentucky	KY Rev. Stat. Ann. §199.520(4)(a) (Michie/Bobbs-Merrill 1991)	Prior to or upon issuance of final decree of adoption.
Maine	ME Rev. Stat. Ann. tit. 19, §533 (West Supp. 1991)	Prior to or upon issuance of final decree of adoption.
North Carolina	NC Gen. Stat. §48-25(e) (1991)	Prior to or upon issuance of final decree of adoption.
Oregon	OR Rev. Stat. §109.342(4) (1991)	Prior to or upon issuance of final decree of adoption.
Texas	TX Fam. Code Ann. §16.032(f) (West Supp. 1992)	"As early as practicable prior to the first meeting of the adoptive parents with the child being placed for adoption."
Utah	UT Code Ann. §78-30-17(1) (1992)	Prior to or upon issuance of final decree of adoption.
Washington	WA Rev. Code Ann. §26.33.380 (West Supp. 1992)	Prior to the adoptive placement.

Table 23 ◆ States That Permit Nonidentifying Information to Be Updated

State	Statute	Type of Requirement
Arizona	AZ Rev. Stat. Ann. §8-129(B)(2) (1989)	Information "may be supplemented" by any member of the birth family, any member of the adoptive family, or any adult adoptee of the family of an adult adoptee.
Connecticut	CT Gen. Stat. Ann. §45a-746 (West Supp. 1992)	"Any genetic parent...may add... updated information" to the information gathered initially in the genetic parent's medical and social history.
Georgia	GA Code Ann. §19-8-23(d) (Michie 1991)	Agency may petition court to obtain access to record "for purpose of adding subsequently obtained medical information."
Indiana	IN Code Ann. §31-3-4-14 (Burns 1987 and Supp. 1991)	The state registrar "shall supplement the medical history with medical information received from any person."
Kansas	KS Stat. Ann. §59-2130 (Supp. 1991)	"The secretary of social and rehabilitation services shall adopt rules and regulations establishing procedures for updating a child's genetic, medical and social history if new information becomes known at a later date."
Michigan	MI Comp. Laws Ann. §710.68 (West Supp. 1992)	If a child-placing agency, court, or the department "receives written information concerning a physician-verified medical or genetic condition of a person biologically related to an adoptee," the information is to be conveyed to the adoptee or adoptive parent(s) and the information is to be placed in the adoption file.
Minnesota	MN Stat. Ann. §259.47 (West 1987 and Supp. 1992)	"When the agency receives information about a medical or genetic condition which has affected or may affect the physical or mental health of genetically related persons, the agency shall make a diligent effort to contact those persons in order to transmit health information."

Table 23 ◆ (continued)

State	Statute	Type of Requirement
New Mexico	NM Stat. Ann. §40-7-53 (Michie 1989)	"At any time, a biological parent may file information regarding his location or changes in background information, whether medical or social."
North Dakota	ND Cent. Code §14-15-16 (1991)	The child-placing agency "may inform the adopted adult or the adoptive parents of a minor of the death of a genetic parent;" "may inform the genetic parents of pertinent medical information concerning the adopted child or adult;" and "may inform the adopted adult or the adoptive parents of a minor of pertinent medical information concerning the genetic parents."
Ohio	OH Rev. Code Ann. §3107.12(D)(4) (Anderson 1989)	"A biological parent or a person other than a biological parent who provided information in the preparation of the social or medical histories of the biological parents of a minor may cause...the histories to be corrected or expanded to include different or additional types of information."
Pennsylvania	PA Stat. Ann. tit. 23, §2905(d)(2) (Supp. 1992)	"The natural parents shall be entitled to update...records, as necessary, to reflect the natural parent's current address or any other information pertaining to the natural parents."
Texas	TX Fam. Code Ann. §16.032 (West Supp. 1992)	"The department, authorized agency, parent, guardian, person, or entity who prepares or files the original report is required to furnish supplemental medical, psychological, and psychiatric information to the adoptive parents should it become available, and to file such supplemental information where the original report is filed, where it shall be retained for as long as the original report is required to be retained."

Table 23 ◆ **(continued)**

State	Statute	Type of Requirement
West Virginia	WV Code §48-4-10 (Supp. 1991)	"Either birth parent may from time to time submit additional social, medical, or genetic history for the adoptee, which information shall be placed in the court file by the clerk, who shall bring the existence of this medical information to the attention of the court."
Wisconsin	WI Stat. Ann. §48.432 (West Supp. 1991)	"If the department or another agency that maintains records relating to the adoption of an adoptee receives a report from a physician stating that a birth parent or another offspring of the birth parent has acquired or may have a genetically transferable disease, the department or agency shall notify the adoptee and the adoptee's parent(s), and shall notify the birth parent if either receives a physician's report that the adoptee has such a condition."

Table 24   ◆ States with Statutes That Permit Disclosure of Updated Information

State	Statute	Circumstances under Which Disclosure May Occur
Arizona	AZ Rev. Stat. Ann. §8-129(B)(3) (1989)	Upon request of any person entitled to disclosure.
Connecticut	CT Gen. Stat. Ann. §45a-746 (West Supp. 1992)	Upon request of any person entitled to disclosure.
Florida	FL Stat. Ann. §63.162(f) (West Supp. 1992)	Upon request of adoptee after he or she reaches majority.
Georgia	GA Code Ann. §19-8-23 (Michie 1991)	Only upon court order after agency petitions court and demonstrates necessity for information because of medical emergency or diagnosis.
Michigan	MI Comp. Laws Ann. §710.68 (West Supp. 1992)	Agency required to take affirmative steps to notify adoptee or other designated individual in life-threatening situations; otherwise, only upon request.
Minnesota	MN Stat. Ann. §§259.47 (West Supp. 1992)	Agency must make "diligent effort" to contact concerned individuals to provide information about medical or genetic condition that may affect physical or mental health; on consent of party, agency to provide information about nature of death or terminal illness of birth parent or adoptee.
New Mexico	NM Stat. Ann. §40-7-53 (D) (Michie 1988)	Upon application to clerk of court.
North Dakota	ND Cent. Code §14-15-16(3) (1991)	Upon written request of adult adoptee.
Ohio	OH Rev. Code Ann. §3107.17(D) (Anderson 1989)	Inspection by adopted person or adoptive parents permitted upon request to clerk of court.
Texas	TX Fam. Code Ann. §16.032(l) (West Supp. 1992)	Agency required to supply supplemental information to adoptive parents.

Table 24   ◆ (continued)

State	Statute	Circumstances under Which Disclosure May Occur
Wisconsin	WI Stat. Ann. §48.432 (West 1987 and Supp. 1991)	Generally, on request; if agency or department obtains information on genetically transferred diseases, it must communicate the information to the minor adoptee's adoptive parents or to adult adoptee.

Table 25 ◆ States That Have Central Adoption Registries for Maintenance of Information

State	Statute	Registry Site
Alabama	AL Code §26-10A-31 (Supp. 1991)	State department of human resources.
Alaska	AK Stat. §18.50.500(a) (1991)	State registrar who is required to attach information to original birth certificate.
Arizona	AZ Rev. Stat. Ann. §8-129 (B)(1) (1989)	The division, agencies or person placing the child; any agency that ceases to function must transfer records to the division.
Indiana	IN Code Ann. §§31-3-1-2, -4-12 to -4-15 (Burns 1987 and Supp. 1991)	State registrar.
Kansas	KS Stat. Ann. §59-2130 (Supp. 1991)	Secretary of social and rehabilitation services.
Louisiana	LA Rev. Stat. CH.C. Art. 1270-1278 (West 1991)	Department of social services.
Nebraska	NE Rev. Stat. §43-107 (Supp. 1990)	Bureau of vital statistics of the department of health.
North Carolina	NC Gen. Stat. §48-24 (1991)	Department of human resources.
Texas	TX Fam. Code Ann. §16.032 (West Supp. 1992)	The department or authorized agency placing the child for adoption; if an agency ceases to function, it must transfer records to the department; any non-agency adoption intermediary must file a copy of all medical and social history reports and supplemental information with the department.
Utah	UT Code Ann. §78-30-17 (1992)	Bureau of vital statistics of the department of health.
Wisconsin	WI Stat. Ann. §48.432 (West Supp. 1991)	Department of health and human services.

Table 26 ◆ States with Statutes That Impose Liability for Failing to Meet Disclosure Requirements

State	Statute	Nature of Enforcement Provision
Indiana	IN Code Ann. §31-3-4-19 (Burns 1987 and Supp. 1991)	Provides penalties as a Class A misdemeanor for knowingly transmitting false information regarding medical history, for disclosing information beyond that permitted by statute, and for allowing an employee to commit those violations recklessly, knowingly, or intentionally.
Iowa	IA Code Ann. §600.8(11) (West 1981 and Supp. 1992)	Creates a misdemeanor and criminal sanctions for "any person who assists in or impedes the placement or adoption of a minor person" in violation of the statutory requirements for placement, investigation, and disclosure of medical background information.
Louisiana	LA Rev. Stat. Ch. C. Art. 1186 (West 1991)	Imposes a fine of "not more than 500 dollars" or imprisonment "for not more than 90 days, or both" for violation of confidentiality requirements.

Table 27 ◆ States That Limit Liability for Failing to Comply with Disclosure Requirements

State	Statute	Provision
Georgia	GA Code Ann. §19-8-23 (Michie 1991)	No civil or criminal liability when department or agency employee "releases information or makes authorized contacts in good faith" and in compliance with statute.
Illinois	IL Ann. Stat. ch. 40, ¶1522.5 (Smith-Hurd Supp. 1992)	No liability for "acts or efforts made within the scope of the Act."
North Dakota	ND Cent. Code §14-15-16(14) (1991)	"Any child-placing agency discharging in good faith its responsibility under this section is immune from any liability, civil or criminal, that otherwise might result."
Wisconsin	WI Stat. Ann. §48.432(8) (West 1987 and Supp. 1991)	Civil and criminal immunity granted for persons who comply with the disclosure provisions "in good faith."

Conclusion

Two important issues for child welfare agencies that provide adoption services are the emergence of the tort of wrongful adoption and the growing interest of state legislatures in regulating the disclosure of nonidentifying health and background information about children who are placed with adoptive families. Agencies providing adoption services must recognize that courts increasingly have become active in the area of wrongful adoption and have held that intentional misrepresentation, deliberate concealment, and negligent disclosure of information regarding the child's history or prognosis will subject an agency to legal liability. At the same time, states are imposing disclosure requirements through state law. These requirements define the duty to disclose, the extent of required disclosure, and the liability that will be imposed for failure to comply with disclosure requirements. Agencies can best respond to judicial and statutory requirements through an understanding of these requirements and an adherence to high standards of practice.